# Concordance of Querida Amazonia

This concordance presents all the words in *Querida Amazonia*. It lists the paragraph numbers in which each word is used. If a word entry contains multiple entries for the same paragraph number, it means that the paragraph contains multiple entries of that word. The footnotes were not included in the concordance. Words with an apostrophe were considered a separate entry from their non-possessive versions. Additional entries have been created to differentiate the occasional word. The concordance is based upon the English translation provided by Liberia Editrice Vaticana on the Holy See website. Titles of books or names of people are often given a brief description. The books of the Bible referenced with in text citations have been identified. Words in the title were included as paragraph [0].

Sincerely, The Saint Joseph's Concordance Series Collection Team

Evann Yakabuski – General Editor
Ethann Yakabuski – Programming

Other Concordances Published by the Editors include:

Concordance of Vatican II: All 16 Major Documents

Concordance of Texts on Clerical Abuse

Concordance of John Paul's Theology of the Body: All 129 Audiences

Concordance of *Fratelli Tutti*

Concordance of *Laudato Si'*

Concordance of *Humanae Vitae*

Concordance of *Lumen Fidei*

Concordance of *Pacem in Terris*

Concordance of *Marialis Cultus*

Concordance of *Casti Connubii*

Concordance of Saint John Paul II: Volume I - Consisting of 11 Encyclicals

Please Visit

*stjosephsconcordances.wordpress.com*

For updates, suggestions, and our contact page.

## Table of Contents

# Letter A

**a** :
[2][2][2][5][5][5][5][6][6][7][8][8][8][9]
[9][11][11][12][12][12][13][13][14][14]
[15][16][16][17][17][17][18][19][20][20]
[20][20][20][20][20][21][22][22][22][22]
[23][23][24][24][24][24][26][26][26][27]
[27][27][27][27][27][27][28][29][30][30]
[30][31][31][31][31][31][31][31][31][31]
[32][32][33][33][33][33][33][33][33][34]
[35][35][35][36][36][37][37][37][37][37]
[37][37][39][39][39][40][40][40][41][41]
[41][41][41][42][42][42][42][43][43][43]
[45][45][45][46][46][47][47][47][47][47]
[48][48][48][48][48][48][48][49][49][49]
[50][51][51][52][52][52][53][53][54][55]
[55][55][56][57][57][58][59][59][61][61]
[61][63][63][63][63][64][64][64][65][66]
[66][66][66][66][67][67][67][67][68][68]
[68][68][68][68][68][69][69][69][69][69]
[70][70][70][70][71][71][71][71][71][72]
[72][72][72][73][73][73][73][73][74][74]
[74][75][75][75][75][76][76][76][77][77]
[77][78][78][78][78][78][79][79][79][79]
[79][80][80][81][81][81][81][81][82][82]
[83][84][84][84][84][84][85][86][86][86]
[87][87][88][88][88][89][90][92][93][93]
[93][93][93][94][94][94][94][95][95][95]
[97][98][98][98][100][100][101][101]
[101][101][101][101][101][102][103]
[103][103][103][103][104][104][104]
[105][105][107][107][107][107][107]
[108][111][111]

**abandon** : [18][111]

**abandoned** : [63][84]

**abandonment** : [52]

**abhorrence** : [15]

**abilities** : [17][90]

**ability** : [71][108]

**able** : [46][51][66][69][96]

**aboriginal** : [71][83]

**abounds** : [49]

**about** : [24][33][37][39][49][51][58]
[68][83][108]

**above** : [33][59][64][88][108]

**absolve** : [88]

**absurd** : [15]

**abundant** : [48][91]

**abuse** : [15][42][42][42][111]

**abused** : [56]

**abusers** : [18]

**accept** : [59][107][107][108]

**acceptance** : [84]

**accepted** : [67][105]

**access** : [14][103]

**accessible** : [84]

**accompanied** : [14][75]

**accompaniment** : [92]

**accompany** : [21]

**accomplished** : [100]

**accordance** : [105]

**account** : [15]

**accumulating** : [71]

**achieve** : [70]

**acknowledge** : [5][15][35][53][63]

acknowledged : [27]

acknowledgment : [22]

acquire : [90][105]

acquired : [12][58]

act : [106]

acted : [99]

action : [70]

actions : [33]

active : [40][94][102]

activity : [43][54]

actors : [11]

acts : [12]

adapt : [32]

add : [12]

addition : [50][51][54]

addressed : [107]

addressing : [5][67]

admire : [56]

admired : [57]

admitted : [100]

adoration : [101]

adorns : [68]

advance : [30][111]

advanced : [7]

advancement : [75][75]

advances : [29][45][52]

advantage : [79]

aesthetic : [56]

affected : [11]

affecting : [14]

affection : [5]

affects : [33][39][42]

African : [9][32]

after : [26][111]

again : [27][64][64]

against : [12][18][19]

age : [15]

agencies : [50]

ago : [78]

agreeing : [25]

agreements : [13]

agriculture : [17]

a-historic : [37]

aid : [92]

aim : [93]

aimed : [13]

air : [42][43]

albeit : [79]

algae : [49]

alien : [11]

**alienating** : [76]

**alight** : [44]

**alive** : [34][39][66][99][111]

**all** : [0][1][2][8][13][14][18][19][21][21]
[22][24][33][33][36][41][41][44][48][52]
[55][57][59][62][64][64][65][71][72][73]
[74][74][74][82][82][86][87][87][88][90]
[107][107][108][108][109][109][110]
[111][111][111][111][111][111][111]

**alleged** : [36]

**allow** : [14][72][103][105][111]

**allowed** : [29]

**allowing** : [68]

**alluvium** : [48]

**almost** : [59]

**alone** : [10][76][87][88]

**along** : [15][45][82][111]

**alongside** : [18][41][61][78]

**already** : [39][58][66][68][78][94][100]

**also** : [5][5][8][13][15][18][27][30][37]
[41][45][46][48][48][48][49][50][51][52]
[54][59][60][63][66][66][67][69][71][72]
[72][74][77][78][85][86][90][91][93][94]
[98][103][107][111]

**altered** : [14]

**alternation** : [43]

**alternative** : [39]

**alternatives** : [17][51]

**although** : [35][49][87]

**always** : [8][16][19][39][41][43][51][58]
[69][69][79][98]

**am** : [5][5][15][35]

**Amazon** : [1][1][2][3][4][4][5][6][7][7]
[7][7][8][8][10][10][12][12][12][14][15]
[15][16][16][18][19][20][24][24][26][26]
[26][28][29][31][32][33][35][36][38][40]
[41][41][41][42][43][44][45][45][45][46]
[47][48][48][48][48][48][49][50][51][52]
[55][55][56][57][57][57][58][60][61][61]
[61][62][64][65][66][69][70][70][71][75]
[76][78][78][81][84][85][89][90][92][94]
[95][96][97][98][99][101][102][102]
[105][107][108][110][110][111][111]
[111][111][111][111]

**Amazonas** : [43][44]

**Amazonia (as in Querida Amazonia)** :
[0][9][45][95][111]

**Amazonian** : [7][8][19][24][28][34][35]
[48][61][66][76][77][77][86][86][89][90]
[94][97][98][103][106]

**amen** : [111]

**America** : [19][61][65][67][90]

**American** : [97]

**amid** : [18][21][45][46][106]

**among** : [20][82][97]

**ample** : [11]

**amputated** : [15]

**an** : [1][7][7][7][8][8][8][8][10][11][12]
[12][14][15][15][17][18][20][22][30][30]
[35][37][40][40][42][43][45][48][49][49]
[56][56][58][58][60][61][63][67][71][73]
[76][76][77][79][79][79][80][85][85][93]
[105][106]

**anacondas** : [46]

**analyze** : [55]

**ancestors** : [42]

**ancestral** : [40][51][70]

**Anchieta (as in Saint Joseph of Anchieta)** : [65]

**ancient** : [45][56][69]

**and** : [0][1][1][2][2][2][2][3][3][4][4][4]
[4][5][5][5][5][5][7][7][7][7][7][7][8][8]
[8][8][9][9][9][9][9][9][10][10][11][11]
[11][11][12][12][12][12][13][13][13][13]
[13][14][14][14][14][14][14][14][14][14]
[14][14][14][14][14][15][15][15][15][15]
[15][15][15][16][16][16][16][16][17][17]
[17][17][17][17][17][18][18][18][18][18]
[18][19][19][19][19][20][20][20][20][20]
[20][20][21][21][21][21][21][21][22][22]
[22][22][22][22][22][23][23][23][24][24]
[24][24][24][26][26][26][26][26][26][27]
[27][27][27][27][29][29][29][29][30][30]
[30][30][30][30][31][31][31][31][31][31]
[31][32][32][32][32][32][32][32][32][32]
[33][33][33][33][33][33][33][34][34][34]
[34][35][35][35][35][35][35][36][37]
[37][37][37][37][38][38][39][39][39][39]
[40][40][40][40][40][40][41][41][41][41]
[41][42][42][42][42][42][42][42][42][42]
[42][42][43][43][43][43][44][44][45][45]
[45][45][45][45][45][45][46][46][46][46]
[46][46][47][47][47][48][48][48][48][48]
[48][48][49][49][49][50][50][50][50][50]
[51][51][51][51][51][51][52][52][52][52]
[52][52][53][53][53][53][53][54][55][55]
[55][55][56][56][56][56][56][57][57][57]
[57][57][57][58][58][58][58][58][58][58]
[59][59][60][60][60][61][61][61][61][62]
[62][62][62][63][63][63][63][63][63][64]
[64][64][64][64][64][64][65][65][65][66]
[66][66][67][67][67][68][68][68][69][69]
[69][70][70][70][70][71][71][71][71][71]
[71][71][71][71][72][72][72][72][72][72]
[72][73][73][73][73][73][73][74][74][74]
[74][74][74][75][75][75][76][76][76][76]
[76][76][77][77][77][77][77][78][78][78]
[78][79][79][79][79][79][80][80][80][80]
[81][81][81][82][82][82][82][82][83][83]
[83][83][83][83][84][84][84][84][84][84]
[84][84][85][85][85][85][85][86][86][87]
[87][88][88][89][89][89][89][90][90][90]
[90][91][91][91][91][92][92][92][93][93]
[93][94][94][94][94][94][94][95][95][95]
[95][96][96][97][98][98][98][98][98][98]
[98][98][98][99][99][99][99][99][100]
[100][101][101][101][101][101][101]
[102][102][102][102][103][103][103]
[103][104][104][104][104][104][105]
[105][105][105][105][105][105][106]
[106][106][106][107][107][107][107]
[108][108][108][108][108][108][109]
[109][109][109][109][110][110][111]
[111][111][111][111][111][111][111]
[111][111][111][111][111][111]

**Andes** : [45]

**animal** : [54]

**animals** : [31][47]

**announce** : [64]

**another** : [26][26][32][58][64][64]
[91][106]

**answer** : [50][87]

**answers** : [105]

**anxious** : [58]

**any** : [26][36][37][37][40][43][65][91]

**anything** : [23]

**Aparecida** : [61][86][97]

**apart** : [104]

**apostolic** : [0][68]

**apparently** : [104]

**appeal** : [63]

**appealed** : [22]

**appears** : [101]

**application** : [61]

**applies** : [97]

**apply** : [2][4]

**apportioned** : [20]

**appreciate** : [21][40][55][72][108][111]

**appreciation** : [60]

**approach** : [8][8][71][100][101]

**approaches** : [104][105]

**appropriate** : [14][90]

**arduous** : [8]

**are** : [9][9][9][10][11][11][14][14][15]
[17][17][19][20][20][20][24][24][26][26]
[26][27][28][28][29][29][32][32][32][33]
[33][35][35][35][37][42][42][43][44][45]
[45][49][52][57][57][57][58][58][58][59]
[61][62][72][72][72][73][76][78][79][81]
[81][83][83][85][87][88][89][92][98][99]
[102][105][105][105][105][109][109]
[109][109][109][109][109][109]

**area** : [5][69]

**areas** : [5][20]

**arguments** : [32]

**arise** : [78]

**arisen** : [45]

**arises** : [101]

**arose** : [40]

**around** : [37]

**arrive** : [72][98]

**arrived** : [16]

**artistic** : [35]

**arts** : [35]

**as** : [5][8][10][12][12][12][12][12][12]
[13][14][14][15][15][15][16][17][17][19]
[19][20][20][21][21][23][24][25][25][26]
[27][27][27][28][29][32][32][32][32][34]
[35][35][36][37][39][46][46][47][48][48]
[48][48][52][53][53][56][56][57][62][62]
[65][66][69][69][69][71][71][72][73][74]
[76][78][78][79][80][80][83][92][95][96]
[99][101][101][101][105][105][107]
[108][108][109]

**ashamed** : [62]

**ashes** : [66]

**aside** : [62]

**ask** : [19][26][64][111][111]

**asked** : [86]

**aspect** : [48]

**aspects** : [36][68]

**assembly** : [4]

**assigning** : [105]

**assist** : [5]

**assistance** : [25]

**assisting** : [72]

**associations** : [97]

**assume** : [92]

**astonishingly** : [45]

at : [2][3][11][13][17][17][19][22][25][25][26][26][30][31][38][55][61][61][67][73][76][76][79][80][86][86][87][88][88][90][91][94][99][102][104][107][107][108][111][111]

attained : [77]

attempt : [21][79][107]

attention : [25][50][67]

attentive : [108]

attested : [96]

attitude : [67]

attitudes : [90]

austere : [18][71]

authentic : [37][63][66][71][96][105]

authentically : [17]

authoritative : [26]

authorities : [14]

authority : [87][94]

autonomy : [67]

avoid : [32][48]

awaits : [43]

awaken : [5][55][56][93]

awakens : [105]

away : [13][80][83][84][109]

awe : [111]

axis : [45]

# Letter B

back : [15][82]

backgrounds : [33]

balance : [48]

banner : [37]

banquet : [109]

baptized : [33][99]

barren : [37]

base : [96]

based : [39][52][68]

basic : [51]

basin : [12][97]

basis : [20][32]

bathing : [45]

be : [4][7][8][9][12][12][12][12][13][14][17][17][17][17][19][25][26][26][26][27][27][27][27][28][28][28][29][30][31][35][35][37][37][37][37][40][40][40][41][41][41][42][42][46][48][48][49][50][51][53][56][56][57][58][59][61][61][62][63][63][65][65][68][69][69][69][71][71][72][72][72][72][73][75][78][78][79][80][80][81][82][82][84][84][84][85][86][87][87][87][88][89][89][90][90][90][92][93][94][94][94][98][98][100][103][106][106][108][108][111][111]

bear : [33]

bearers : [29][35]

bears : [66]

**blending** : [37]

**blessed** : [111]

**blessings** : [80]

**blood** : [31][42][47][96][109]

**blossom** : [31]

**blows** : [20]

**blur** : [33]

**bodies** : [20]

**body** : [46][63][88]

**bolder** : [105]

**boldness** : [94][95][105][105]

**Bolivia** : [5]

**bondage** : [41]

**bonds** : [55]

**borders** : [97]

**born** : [45][45][72][73][77]

**Borneo** : [48]

**both** : [8][52][90][104]

**boundaries** : [14][52]

**boundless** : [63]

**brazil** : [5]

**Brazilian** : [16]

**breaks** : [101]

**breasts** : [15]

**breeze** : [20]

**bride** : [6][101]

**bridge** : [37]

**brief** : [2][6][64]

**briefly** : [5]

**bring** : [18][21][28][33][62][111]

**bringing** : [34][58]

**brings** : [66][76]

**broad** : [60][85][94]

**broaden** : [100]

**broader** : [105]

**broken** : [22]

**brothers** : [7][41][42]

**build** : [17][20][109]

**built** : [89]

**burst** : [47][47]

**business** : [50]

**businesses** : [14][14][14]

**but** : [5][8][8][10][10][15][15][15][17][19][21][27][28][28][28][30][30][31][38][41][41][45][50][52][55][59][61][63][66][66][66][67][69][69][69][72][73][76][76][77][78][83][87][89][90][91][92][94][95][100][101][109][111]

**buy** : [59]

**by** : [1][4][5][10][11][11][14][21][21][24][25][27][31][33][36][37][37][37][42][42][45][45][47][48][54][57][59][61][62][64][72][75][75][77][77][78][78][80][81][84][84][90][96][99][99][101][105][105][105][106][106][108][109][109][109]

[109][109][109][109][109][109][109]
[110][111][111][111][111][111][111]

# Letter C

call : [62][93][111]

called : [14][19][26][27][41][61][66]
[72][73][76][77][82][83][84][99][109]

calls : [8][52][57][109]

came : [18]

can : [2][2][5][6][7][7][7][8][17][19]
[25][26][33][33][35][37][37][37][40][41]
[52][55][55][55][55][58][58][59][62][62]
[63][63][67][68][69][72][72][72][78][79]
[81][82][82][84][85][86][88][88][88][89]
[89][90][93][94][94][103][104][106][108
][110][110][111][111][111]

cannot : [14][19][50][58][59][62][63]
[85][87][92][98][108]

canoe : [31]

canoes : [46]

capable : [7][22][33][58][59][95][106]

capacity : [20][22]

capital : [44]

capitulating : [50]

carbon : [48]

care : [33][41][41][42][42][42][42]
[71][71][80][101][110][111][111]

caring : [32][41]

carnage : [17]

carries : [50]

carry : [43][85]

carrying : [53]

cascade : [20]

case : [27][34][89][107]

cases : [96]

cast : [75]

catastrophic : [59]

catchword : [84]

catechized : [99]

categories : [31][68]

cathedral : [111]

Catholic : [60]

Catholicism : [78]

Catholics : [107]

caught : [43]

celebrate : [89][93]

celebrated : [91]

celebrates : [88][101]

celebration : [38][86][88][89][89][111]

celebrations : [20][83]

central : [103]

centred : [65][80]

centuries : [16][30][34][66][99]

century : [12][15]

**certain** : [13][14][78][78][89]

**certainly** : [73][80]

**cf** : [15][15][15][52]

**challenge** : [17][77][98]

**challenged** : [4]

**challenges** : [5][33][35][67][94][104][105]

**change** : [58]

**changed** : [16][58]

**changing** : [78][78]

**chapter** : [7][27][40][60][64]

**character** : [70][87]

**characterized** : [106]

**characterizes** : [74]

**charge** : [33]

**charged** : [15][79]

**charisms** : [91][94][102]

**charity** : [22][65][65][72]

**cheerful** : [77]

**chestnut** : [9]

**child** : [31][73]

**children** : [11][12][15][54][80][84]

**choices** : [27]

**chose** : [82][101]

**Christ** : [6][22][22][41][62][63][64][64][69][74][75][80][87][87][87][101][109]

[111][111]

**Christ's** : [65][87]

**Christian** : [7][65][65][66][74][75][81][83][88][89][105][107][107]

**Christianity** : [69][69]

**Christians** : [25][27][57][62][96][108][109]

**Christus (as in *Christus Vivit*)** : [64]

**Church** : [1][4][6][7][19][19][25][33][60][61][61][61][66][66][66][67][67][68][68][69][69][69][70][72][76][77][84][84][84][85][85][87][87][89][94][94][94][95][99][100][100][101][101][101][101][103]

**Churches** : [97][97]

**Church's** : [5][75][91][96]

**circumstances** : [89]

**cite** : [3]

**cities** : [10][10][10][21][30][30][58][72]

**city** : [32][72]

**civil** : [24][50]

**civilization** : [29][37][109]

**claim** : [2][111]

**clear** : [8][20][42][52][57][75]

**clericalize** : [100]

**climate** : [48]

**clip** : [69]

**close** : [31][41][72][84][98]

concerns : [2][12][79][82]

conclude : [107][111]

concluded : [1]

conclusion : [87][110]

conclusions : [3][32]

concrete : [84][105][111]

concretely : [2][94]

condemned : [12]

conference : [61]

confers : [74]

confessions : [107]

confidence : [24]

confident : [67]

configuration : [95]

configure : [86]

configures : [87]

conflict : [104][104]

conflicts : [103]

confronting : [5]

congo : [48]

connect : [76]

connected : [41]

connection : [75]

conquer : [73]

conquest : [19][48]

consciences : [53]

conscious : [41][55]

consciousness : [15][42]

consecrated : [4][95][95][98]

consensus : [27]

consent : [14][51]

consequences : [23][23][51][59]

consequently : [36][84][93][98][104]

consider : [85][111]

considered : [12][48][79][87]

considering : [79]

consists : [65]

consoling : [111]

constant : [40][98]

constantly : [53][64][66][66][78]

constitute : [65]

construction : [11]

consume : [59]

consumerism : [36][58][72]

consumerist : [33][46][59][108]

consumption : [53]

contact : [35][40][80][82][108]

contain : [107]

contains : [48][48]

contemplate : [55]

**create** : [69][108]

**created** : [41][42][57]

**creates** : [45]

**creating** : [68]

**creation** : [42][42][60][64][73][74][81][81][81][82][82][110][111]

**creative** : [2][98]

**creativity** : [95][105]

**Creator** : [42][52]

**creature** : [101]

**creatures** : [57][74][111]

**cries** : [57]

**crime** : [8][14]

**crimes** : [19][19]

**critical** : [49][50][67]

**crucial** : [49]

**crucified** : [64]

**cruelty** : [15]

**cry** : [8][8][9][10][19][46][48][52][52][52][52][56][57][62]

**culmination** : [82]

**cultivate** : [28][32][107]

**cultural** : [7][14][22][27][30][30][31][34][35][35][35][36][36][37][37][37][38][39][40][41][67][69][69][72][85]

**culturally** : [28]

**culture** : [13][20][22][24][37][40][58][61][67][67][67][68][68][68][68][68][68][69][78][78][94]

**cultures** : [17][22][28][29][30][33][36][36][36][38][39][39][40][40][45][60][66][70][81][86][90][94][105][111]

**curia** : [3]

**curing** : [48]

**current** : [15]

**customs** : [35][40]

**cut** : [15][42]

**cycles** : [48]

# Letter D

**daily** : [41][41][80][83]

**damaged** : [35][40]

**damages** : [39]

**dampening** : [105]

**dance** : [46][82]

**danger** : [49][80]

**dangers** : [46]

**dark** : [111]

**darker** : [36]

**daughters** : [57][111]

**day** : [33]

**days** : [43][73][105]

**dazzling** : [48]

**destroyed** : [111]

**destroys** : [46]

**destruction** : [13][15][17][42][59]

**detached** : [20]

**determine** : [87]

**determines** : [43]

**determining** : [43]

**devastation** : [12]

**develop** : [23][38][58][61][89]

**developed** : [12][29][36][36][40]

**developing** : [17][26]

**development** : [13][17][40][58][76][90][92]

**develops** : [32][87]

**devote** : [63]

**devoted** : [95]

**devotion** : [89][99][107]

**diagnoses** : [11]

**dialogue** : [2][25][26][26][26][26][27][37][37][38][66][90][95][101][108]

**did** : [12][15][15][19][105][109]

**differ** : [32]

**differences** : [37][106]

**different** : [22][29][30][38][38][45][60][64][81][87][89][94][104]

**differentiated** : [97]

**differently** : [106]

**difficult** : [69][84]

**difficulties** : [80]

**dignified** : [17][46][76][80]

**dignifies** : [76]

**dignify** : [63]

**dignity** : [7][12][12][18][21][30][63][63]

**dimension** : [58][71][76][83]

**diminish** : [100]

**diminishing** : [20][33]

**dioxide** : [48]

**dire** : [30][72]

**direct** : [42]

**directed** : [17]

**directing** : [57][82]

**direction** : [103]

**directly** : [60]

**disappear** : [29]

**disappearance** : [54]

**disaster** : [8]

**discarded** : [30][75][84]

**discernment** : [2]

**disciples** : [65][96]

**discipline** : [84]

[40][42][60][60]

**dreams** : [4][6][111]

**drink** : [34]

**driven** : [72]

**drives** : [30]

**drove** : [30]

**drug** : [14]

**dry** : [48]

**due** : [30][85]

**dull** : [53]

**dulled** : [15]

**duplicate** : [2]

**during** : [1][2][11][15][19][111]

**duty** : [26][107]

**dwell** : [111]

**dwellers** : [32]

**dwelt** : [9]

# Letter E

**each** : [6][22][23][27][31][32][32][40][48][50][54][54][57][68][77][91][104]

**earlier** : [2][29]

**earliest** : [105]

**Earth** : [42][42]

**earth** : [8][42][47][48][52][70]

[70][71][82]

**easily** : [16][49][56]

**east** : [43]

**easy** : [37]

**ecclesial** : [6][25][60][64][72][85][85][94][97][103][104]

**ecclesiastical** : [25]

**ecological** : [8][8][35][40][57]

**ecology** : [1][41][41][41][41][41][41][58][58][58]

**economic** : [11][14][25][49][50][50][52]

**economy** : [33][39]

**ecosystem** : [48]

**ecosystems** : [22][42][49][52][71]

**Ecuador** : [5][22]

**ecumenical** : [105]

**education** : [12][17][28][51][57][93]

**educational** : [58][60]

**effect** : [33]

**effective** : [100][103]

**effectively** : [92][98]

**effectiveness** : [23]

**effort** : [8][43][82][89][94]

**efforts** : [20][21][61][86][97]

**Egypt** : [52]

**elders** : [70]

enmity : [108]

enormous : [12][13]

enough : [49][73]

enrich : [26]

enriched : [4][37][106]

enriches : [68][68]

enriching : [106]

enrichment : [30]

enslavement : [10]

ensure : [17][50][52][89][89]

entail : [17][103][103]

entails : [75]

enter : [11][22][56][101]

entering : [65]

entire : [2][4][88]

entirely : [15]

entrusted : [19]

environment : [8][12][14][16][17][21]
[23][40][40][41][41][42][48][48][50][82]

environment's : [48]

environmental : [49]

environmentalism : [8]

envisage : [104]

equals : [26][91]

equilibrium : [48][49]

error : [79]

especially : [15][26][33][33][42][84]
[90][98]

essential : [48][48][49][69][80]

establish : [52][97]

established : [31]

esteem : [22][70][73][107]

esteemed : [27]

eternal : [45][56]

eternity : [44]

ethnic : [35][36]

eucalyptus : [56]

Eucharist : [74][82][82][83][86][86]
[87][88][88][89][89][91][91][92][93]
[101][111]

evaluating : [49]

Evangelii (as in *Evangelii Gaudium*) :
[68]

evangelization : [71][75][96][104]

evangelized : [78][78]

evangelizers : [65][69]

evasiveness : [53]

even : [12][13][14][14][15][15][17][17]
[21][32][35][38][41][47][55][78][86][89]
[96][99][99][102][104][107][107][107]
[108][111]

events : [59]

ever : [12][28][31][74][92][111]

extend : [59]

extent : [51]

extinct : [54]

extinction : [49]

extorted : [18]

extraction : [49]

extreme : [59]

extremes : [43]

eyes : [57]

# Letter F

face : [15][47][61][66][68][72][75][77][101][101][102][104]

faced : [39][111]

faces : [6][7][47][101]

facilitating : [93]

facing : [8]

fact : [13][28][63][87][87][100][103][107]

factors : [36]

fail : [14][50]

failing : [69]

faith : [62][67][67][78][96][99][99][105][109][109]

faithful : [4][18][60][104]

faithfully : [67]

fall : [104]

falling : [72]

falls : [43][45][45]

false : [12]

familial : [20][71]

familiar : [83][94]

families : [39][98]

family : [35][39][70][80]

far : [37][82]

farmhouse : [31]

father : [44]

Father (as in God the Father) : [55][57][57][63][109][111]

Father (as in the Holy Father Francis) : [0]

favour : [27][90]

fear : [45]

fearful : [69]

fearless : [69]

fears : [26]

feast : [111]

features : [7][32][77][77][78][94]

February : [111]

feed : [53]

feel : [14][15][17][20][21][29][55][84][107]

**food** : [89]

**for** : [1][1][2][4][5][5][6][7][8][8][8]
[11][11][11][14][14][15][15][15][15][15]
[16][16][17][19][19][19][20][20][22][22]
[22][23][23][25][25][25][26][26][26][27]
[27][30][32][33][33][33][34][34][35][37]
[37][37][37][39][39][39][40][40][40][41]
[41][41][41][42][42][42][47][47][48][48]
[48][48][49][51][52][52][52][53][54][55]
[56][56][57][57][57][57][58][60][60][61]
[62][63][63][64][65][65][66][67][68][70]
[70][70][71][71][71][72][72][73][74][75]
[75][76][76][76][76][77][78][78][79][80]
[80][82][82][82][82][84][84][84][84][84]
[86][86][88][90][90][92][93][94][98][98]
[99][99][101][106][106][108][109][109]
[109][109][110][111][111][111][111]
[111]

**forced** : [21][39]

**forest** : [11][11][13][14][30][37][42]
[45][45][48][48][48][56]

**forests** : [7][9][10][14][34][35][89][111]

**forever** : [28][31][54]

**forgiveness** : [14][19][88][89]

**forgotten** : [57][57][84]

**form** : [22][32][43][43][69][85][96]

**formation** : [65][90][90][93]

**forms** : [10][13][14][15][26][29][39]
[41][72][73][82][84][102][104][105]

**forth** : [3][7][77][105][109][111]

**forty** : [78]

**foster** : [28][91]

**found** : [35][50][61][64][89][105][105]

**fountain** : [105]

**four** : [6][64]

**fourth** : [60]

**fragility** : [16]

**fragment** : [82]

**fragmentation** : [30]

**fragmented** : [34]

**framework** : [2][22][52]

**Francis (as in the Holy Father Francis)**
: [0]

**Franciscus (as in Pope Francis)** : [111]

**frank** : [108]

**fraternal** : [22][58][65][65]

**fraternity** : [20][22][79][111]

**free** : [14][41][46][109][111]

**freedom** : [10][20][23][52][52]

**French** : [5]

**frenzied** : [72]

**frequent** : [86]

**frequently** : [14][53][98]

**friends** : [62][72][91]

**friendship** : [63]

**from** : [1][3][10][10][10][13][14][15]
[16][16][17][18][18][18][20][20][24][26]
[26][30][31][32][32][33][33][34][34][37]
[37][37][37][40][40][41][43][45][45][45]
[45][45][45][46][46][46][48][53][55][55]
[55][57][62][62][63][63][63][70][72][73]
[73][75][77][78][78][80][80][81][82][86]
[88][89][91][98][98][103][105][105]

[105][105][105][106][111]

**fruit** : [11][33][48]

**fruitful** : [2][68]

**fruits** : [68][70]

**fulfillment** : [71][81]

**fulfills** : [73]

**fulfilment** : [66][76]

**full** : [3][18]

**fullness** : [57]

**fully** : [64][67][67][76][111]

**function** : [87][87]

**functional** : [100][101]

**functioning** : [49]

**functions** : [92]

**fundamental** : [65]

**fundamentally** : [101]

**fungi** : [49]

**further** : [58]

**furthermore** : [39][48]

**future** : [42][71]

# Letter G

**gatherers** : [32]

**gathering** : [79]

**Gaudium (as in *Evangelii Gaudium*)** : [68]

**gave** : [13][15][111]

**gaze** : [111]

**generalizations** : [32]

**generally** : [49]

**generating** : [22]

**generation** : [30][30][78][78]

**generations** : [71]

**generosity** : [105]

**generous** : [7][71][90][96][98][99]

**genuine** : [17]

**geography** : [32]

**gestures** : [82]

**gift** : [16][68][73][74][98][105][105][105]

**gifts** : [48][71][89][91][94][102]

**give** : [13][14][47][51][54][71][73][77]

**given** : [17][21][41][64][68][75][98][111]

**gives** : [27][41][63][109]

**giving** : [7][68]

**global** : [50]

**globalization** : [14][17][17]

**globalized** : [33][39]

**glorious** : [74][109]

glory : [54][111]

go : [2][15][64][82]

goals : [17]

God : [0][1][4][15][19][32][35][41][42]
[52][54][57][57][63][64][66][70][72][73]
[74][74][80][81][82][82][84][95][105]
[109][109][111]

God's : [6][16][52][57][66][68][71][75]
[83][84][89][93]

God-given : [56]

good : [0][4][8][15][15][20][21][26]
[48][49][49][51][71][95][106][108]

goodness : [66]

goods : [33]

Gospel : [18][18][22][61][62][62][64]
[64][65][66][67][68][68][68][69][70][72]
[75][76][76][85]

government : [50]

governments : [50]

grace : [1][6][68][77][81][81][87]
[87][88]

gradual : [79]

gradually : [69]

grant : [4]

granted : [1][100]

grasp : [108]

gratitude : [70]

gratuitousness : [73]

gratuity : [83][83]

grave : [14][18][85]

great : [5][6][10][26][26][32][43][44]
[45][45][48][48][54][61][63][64][65][65]
[70][71][88][91][98][100][107][111]

greater : [23][50][93][100][105][105]

greatest : [65][67][80]

greatly : [52][109][111]

Greco-Roman : [105]

greedy : [58]

green : [45]

grew : [69]

ground : [15][31]

group : [32][40][40][104]

groupings : [32]

groups : [2][21][24][36][37][37][42]
[58][78]

grow : [13][31][33][33][37][61][66][80]
[89][108]

growing : [30][35][35][66][78]

grows : [48]

growth : [28][60][65][92][93][94][97]

guard : [66]

guests : [26]

Guiana : [5]

guide : [2]

guides : [109]

gusts : [43]

Guyana : [5]

# Letter H

habitat : [15]

habitats : [21]

habits : [57][58][58]

had : [15][15][30][30][31][32][101]

hand : [56][68][68]

handed : [66][99]

handing : [78]

handiwork : [111]

hands : [15][73]

happen : [28][53][99]

happening : [47]

happens : [104]

happy : [80]

hard : [31][40]

hardly : [37]

harm : [14][42]

harmonious : [2][95]

harmony : [45][61][71][80]

harvests : [9]

has : [6][8][9][11][12][16][16][19][23]
[23][31][33][33][35][39][39][41][41][42]
[45][48][54][55][56][58][64][66][66][67]
[68][71][73][74][78][84][87][94][95][98]
[98][99][106][111]

have : [2][3][9][9][9][11][13][15][16]
[16][20][22][23][25][26][28][32][34][35]
[35][35][35][36][36][42][42][45][46][51]
[54][54][58][62][62][63][64][69][70][71]
[75][75][76][78][78][79][82][82][95][96]
[96][99][99][100][101][103][103][103]
[107][111]

having : [27]

he : [22][41][41][56][59][67][74][74]
[74][87][87][87][88][88][94][111][111]

head : [46][87][87][88]

heal : [16][21][84]

health : [23][48]

healthy : [13][17][83]

hear : [8][19][64][64]

heard : [7][11][27][28][61]

hearing : [57]

heart : [20][22][41][45][59][62][63][75]
[76][88][111][111]

heartrending : [57]

hearts : [111][111]

heaven : [9][45][82]

heavenly : [57][109]

heed : [86]

heirs : [29]

held : [1]

help : [2][5][46][72][83]

helped : [96]

**helping** : [28][41]

**helplessly** : [13]

**helps** : [45][47][48]

**hence** : [20]

**her** : [9][19][27][60][60][60][60][60]
[60][66][68][68][68][77][84][100][111]

**herding** : [17]

**here** : [11][33][66][68][103]

**heritage** : [33]

**herself** : [19][66][68][72][111]

**hidden** : [44]

**hierarchical** : [87]

**hierarchies** : [38]

**high** : [45]

**higher** : [104][104]

**highest** : [87]

**him** : [62][62][80][87][109]

**himself** : [32][41][57][57][57][57]

**hinge** : [89]

**his** : [27][32][57][57][57][57][62][62]
[62][66][74][74][77][84][87][88][101]
[101][101][101][107][109][109][109]
[110][111][111][111][111][111]

**historical** : [40][105]

**history** : [16][16][19][33][60][66][66]
[69][102]

**holding** : [57]

**holiness** : [76][77][77][77][77][80][85]
[87][93]

**holy (as in the Eucharist)** : [89]

**Holy (as in the Holy Father Francis)** :
[0]

**Holy (as in Holy Orders)** : [87][87][88]
[100][103]

**Holy (as in the Holy Spirit)** : [68][68]
[69][94][99][106]

**home** : [19][48][111]

**homes** : [18]

**hope** : [33][38]

**hopes** : [26][37]

**horizons** : [103][104]

**hospitable** : [48]

**host** : [29]

**hostile** : [21]

**hour** : [111][111]

**how** : [21][21][53][63][69][71][78][78]
[85][101][110][110][111][111][111]

**however** : [5]

**huge** : [50]

**human** : [10][12][12][14][14][15][17]
[20][22][23][23][32][32][33][33][39][40]
[41][41][41][41][49][53][54][57][70][75]
[75][76][80][101]

**humanity** : [7][33][37][41][48][48]

**humanizes** : [76]

**humble** : [46]

# Letter I

[83][87][92][103][108]

**imported** : [31][77]

**impose** : [69]

**imposed** : [40][59]

**imposing** : [84]

**impossible** : [43][59]

**impoverished** : [37][98]

**impoverishment** : [33]

**impressive** : [43]

**impunity** : [13]

**in** : [1][1][2][2][2][3][3][4][5][6][6][6]
[6][7][7][7][8][11][12][12][13][13][14]
[15][15][15][15][16][16][17][17][20][21]
[22][22][22][23][23][24][24][25][26][28]
[28][29][29][30][30][31][31][31][31][32]
[32][32][33][34][35][35][35][35][36][36]
[37][38][39][40][40][41][41][41][41][42]
[42][42][42][43][43][43][43][43][43][43]
[43][45][45][45][48][48][48][49][49][49]
[50][50][50][50][51][51][52][54][54][56]
[56][56][57][57][57][58][58][58][60][61]
[61][61][61][62][63][63][64][64][64][64]
[64][64][65][65][66][66][66][66][66][66]
[66][66][66][66][66][66][67][68][68][68]
[68][68][68][68][69][69][70][70][70][70]
[70][71][71][71][71][71][72][72][72][72]
[73][74][74][74][74][74][74][74][74][75]
[75][76][76][77][77][78][78][78][78][79]
[79][79][80][81][81][81][81][81][81][82]
[82][82][82][82][83][83][84][84][84][84]
[85][85][85][85][86][86][87][87][87][87]
[88][89][89][89][90][90][92][93][93][94]
[94][94][95][95][95][95][96][96][96][97]
[98][98][99][99][100][100][101][101]
[101][101][101][101][102][102][102]
[103][103][103][103][104][104][104]
[105][105][105][105][105][105][105]
[105][106][107][107][107][107][107]
[107][108][108][108][108][109][109]

[111][111][111][111][111][111][111]
[111][111][111][111][111][111][111]
[111][111][111][111][111]

**inalienable** : [50]

**inasmuch** : [72]

**incarnate** : [6][6][6][6][7][60][74][77]
[85]

**incarnation** : [61][69][82][95]

**incidents** : [15]

**include** : [33][70][83]

**including** : [13][24][103]
**incorporated** : [74]

**incorporates** : [83]

**increase** : [10][37][52]

**increasing** : [49]

**increasingly** : [41][66][73][85]

**inculturate** : [82][85]

**inculturated** : [79]

**inculturation** : [65][66][68][69][69][70]
[72][73][74][75][76][78][80][81][84][85]
[85][95][105]

**indeed** : [50][59][65][69][75]

**indies** : [18]

**indifferent** : [80][91]

**indigenism** : [37]

**indigenous** : [9][10][12][14][14][14]
[15][15][15][15][17][18][18][21][24][29]
[32][33][37][39][42][67][71][73][74][79]
[82][82][111]

interaction : [36]

interconnected : [5]

interconnection : [73]

intercultural : [35][38]

interdependence : [73]

interest : [2][12][37][48][55][107]

interests : [9][50][50][50][51][111]

interior : [30][32][36][37][48][56]
[72][98]

internal : [98]

international : [14][50][50]

internationalizing : [50]

interrelationship : [38]

interreligious : [105]

intimate : [40][82]

intimately : [55]

into : [2][22][30][30][31][33][46][46]
[46][46][46][46][48][56][64][65][72][73]
[82][101]

introduced : [78]

intruders : [12]

inured : [15]

invasion : [37][39]

invasive : [28]

invents : [45]

investments : [25]

invite : [5][67]

inviting : [63]

involvement : [40][94]

involves : [41][63][68][71]

involving : [78]

inward-looking : [37]

IPVI : [29]

is : [5][5][8][8][8][8][11][12][13][15]
[15][15][15][17][17][18][19][20][20][20]
[20][22][23][24][26][26][28][28][28][29]
[29][31][33][33][33][34][34][35][37][37]
[37][37][38][39][39][40][40][41][41][41]
[41][41][41][42][42][42][42][43][43][43]
[45][45][45][45][45][45][45][46][46][47]
[47][47][47][48][48][48][48][48][48][48]
[49][49][49][49][50][51][52][52][53][53]
[53][57][57][59][61][64][65][65][66][66]
[66][67][67][69][69][69][69][69][69][73]
[74][74][74][75][78][79][80][81][81][83]
[83][84][84][85][85][86][86][87][87][87]
[87][87][87][87][87][87][87][87][87][87]
[87][88][88][88][88][89][89][90][91][91]
[91][93][94][94][96][98][101][101][103]
[104][104][104][104][105][105][106]
[107][108][108][111][111][111][111]
[111][111]

isolated : [86]

isolation : [29][37][72][85]

Israel : [33]

issues : [2][3][5][50]

issuing : [1]

it : [2][3][3][4][4][5][5][8][8][8][12][12]
[13][13][13][15][15][15][15][16][16][17]
[18][18][20][20][27][28][28][33][34][36]
[37][37][37][38][40][41][42][42][42][43]
[45][45][45][45][45][45][46][46][46][47]

[48][48][48][49][51][52][53][55][55][55]
[55][55][57][59][59][63][64][65][66][67]
[68][68][69][69][73][74][75][75][76][79]
[79][80][82][82][82][84][86][87][87][89]
[90][91][93][94][95][100][103][104]
[104][105][106][107][107][108][108]
[111][111][111][111]

**itinerant** : [98]

**its** : [1][1][1][1][3][7][7][7][8][10][14]
[16][22][24][24][31][31][31][31][31][31]
[32][32][32][32][35][35][35][35][35][42]
[42][43][43][44][45][45][45][45][45][45]
[46][46][46][46][46][46][46][46][46][48]
[48][50][50][56][56][61][66][68][70][70]
[70][72][73][83][85][85][85][89][105]
[105][107][108][108][108][108][111]
[111][111]

**itself** : [28][32][54][85][104][104]

**jealously** : [7]

**jeopardizing** : [15]

# Letter J

**Jesus** : [15][41][57][57][62][64][69]
[74][101][107][109][109][111][111]
[111]

**Jewish** : [105]

**John (as in the Cathedral of Saint John
Lateran)** : [111]

**John (as in Saint John Paul II)** : [67]
[87][111]

**join** : [56][76][104]

**joins** : [56][82]

**joint** : [26]

**Joseph (as in Saint Joseph of Anchieta)**
: [65]

**journey** : [20][61][61][61][69][96]

**joy** : [33][71][80][80]

**joyful** : [71]

**judged** : [84]

**jug** : [31]

**juridical** : [58]

**just** : [20][26][28][43][53][64][91]

**justice** : [8][22][26][52][60][63][69][75]
[77][109][111]

**justify** : [38]

# Letter K

**keep** : [25][47][66][101][102]

**keeping** : [34][39]

**kept** : [13][99]

**kerygma** : [64][65][65][66]

**killing** : [15]

**kind** : [37][101]

**kinds** : [25][93]

**kingdom** : [75][95][109]

**know** : [3][18][54][71][73][73][78][107]
[111][111]

**knowledge** : [33][51][51]

**known** : [12]

knows : [73]

# Letter L

**Laboris** (as in *Instrumentum Laboris*) : [24]

**lack** : [30][34][89]

**laity** : [89][94]

**lakes** : [30]

**lament** : [46][86]

**land** : [5][11][14][20][20][32][32][42][42][48][51][111]

**lands** : [12][14][32][45][66]

**languages** : [39][45][94]

**languish** : [56]

**larger** : [2][58]

**last** : [1][12][15][29][31][43]

**late** : [111]

**Lateran** (as in the Cathedral of Saint John Lateran) : [111]

**Latin** : [61][65][90]

**Laudato** (as in *Laudato Si'*) : [23]

**laws** : [18]

**lay** : [4][92][93][94][94]

**lead** : [59][84][100][100]

**leaders** : [17][94]

**leading** : [18][27]

**leads** : [40][60][65][90]

**learn** : [26][55]

**learned** : [56]

**least** : [7][11][17]

**leather** : [46]

**leaving** : [15][18]

**left** : [48][109]

**legal** : [52]

**legally** : [9]

**legends** : [34]

**legislation** : [18]

**legitimate** : [50][79]

**legs** : [46]

**leisure** : [83]

**length** : [2]

**less** : [19][49][58][58][100]

**lest** : [100]

**let** : [11][15][31][34][37][42][53][56][56][56][69][69][77][78][106][111]

**lets** : [108]

**letting** : [105]

**level** : [23][43][43][76][94][104]

**leveling** : [33]

**liberate** : [63]

**liberator** : [74]

**love** : [3][55][55][57][63][64][71][72][78][101][107][109][111][111]

**loves** : [63][64][73][73][109]

**lovingly** : [33]

**low** : [23]

**lowland** : [45]

**lowlands** : [48]

# Letter M

**made** : [8][21][24][25][25][42][78][86][89][97][101][111]

**maintain** : [67]

**maintaining** : [49][59]

**majority** : [10][16][54]

**make** : [15][27][29][31][33][43][52][100][101]

**makes** : [21][89]

**making** : [101]

**malleable** : [33]

**man** : [31][37][43][45][64][74][101][101]

**management** : [51]

**manifest** : [6]

**manifests** : [32]

**manner** : [43]

**many** : [3][7][9][12][16][18][21][29][29][30][45][45][47][58][60][62][66][70]

[75][78][82][85][86][92][95][96][96][101][102][106][111]

**marginalization** : [17]

**marginalized** : [9][27]

**marine** : [48]

**marked** : [10][36]

**markedly** : [74][75]

**marvel** : [111]

**Mary** : [101][101][107][111][111][111]

**mass** : [39]

**material** : [63][74][74][76]

**maternal** : [71][107][111]

**matter** : [69][82]

**maturation** : [79]

**mature** : [94]

**may** : [4][4][4][52][69][69][91][107][111][111]

**me** : [6][11][37][62][73][73][73][90]

**mean** : [38][76][76][82][92][105]

**meaning** : [13][21][35][63][73][74][74][78][79][79][83]

**means** : [13][14][17][39][39][41][50][57][68][72][72][81][82]

**meant** : [28][87]

**meat** : [11]

**mechanisms** : [33]

**Medellin** : [61]

**models** : [53][77]

**modernity** : [20]

**Mogrovejo** : [65]

**moment** : [102][105]

**money** : [15]

**monkeys** : [9]

**monocultural** : [69]

**monolithic** : [87]

**monotonous** : [69]

**moral** : [24][63]

**more** : [10][12][13][15][15][19][21][21]
[28][30][35][36][41][48][55][55][58][58]
[58][59][60][65][70][76][78][86][89][90]
[92][92][106][111]

**morning** : [20]

**mortgage** : [42]

**Moses** : [15]

**most** : [15][18][26][26][39][48][49][75]
[83][86][87][89][98][103]

**mother** : [42][42][55][84][101][107]
[110][111][111][111][111][111][111]
[111]

**motivating** : [63]

**motivation** : [82]

**mountain** : [45]

**moved** : [99]

**movement** : [68]

**much** : [47][47][71][78][111][111]

**multicultural** : [31]

**multifaceted** : [61]

**multinational** : [5]

**multinationals** : [42]

**multiplicity** : [94]

**multiplied** : [45]

**multitude** : [89]

**museum** : [66]

**musical** : [35]

**must** : [6][6][6][6][8][26][27][27][27]
[40][41][59][61][62][64][64][64][69][72]
[76][84][84][89][90][91][102]

**mutual** : [30][59]

**my** : [2][12][19][20][73][88][111][111]

**myself** : [3]

**mysterious** : [72][74]

**mysteriously** : [57][68]

**mystery** : [1][5][55][82]

**mysticism** : [73][73][73]

**mystique** : [12]

**myth** : [79]

**myths** : [34]

# Letter N

**narrow** : [93][100]

**national** : [14][50]

**nationalities** : [29]

**nations** : [13][13][97]

**native** : [19][82]

**natural** : [7][13][16][17][40][41][50]

**nature** : [20][28][36][41][41][41][42][42][43][46][71][73][81][81][82][82][111]

**near** : [20]

**necessarily** : [75][79]

**necessary** : [66][69][92]

**need** : [8][11][15][15][17][26][33][39][40][41][48][49][52][61][72][72][79][84][86][86][89][90][93][94][106]

**needed** : [69]

**needing** : [12]

**needlessly** : [71]

**needs** : [59][61][62][65][66][70][79][80][95][102][108]

**needy** : [13]

**negative** : [23]

**neglect** : [75][111]

**neither** : [76]

**network** : [97]

**networks** : [17][25][72]

**never** : [9][15][52][54][54][84][105]

**new** : [1][7][14][14][21][22][33][33][52][58][62][65][68][68][68][69][89][93][95][102][104][105][105][109]

**next** : [40][60]

**NGO** : [64]

**night** : [73]

**nine** : [5]

**no** : [9][10][11][12][13][15][19][20][29][54][54][69][89][99][105][108][111]

**noble** : [33]

**nondelegable** : [87]

**nondeterministic** : [31]

**none** : [12][16][108]

**nonetheless** : [49]

**nor** : [2][16][25][37][40][54][63][66][84]

**not** : [2][3][8][10][12][12][15][15][15][16][17][17][17][18][18][19][19][24][26][27][27][28][29][32][32][36][37][37][37][38][38][41][42][42][45][48][48][48][49][50][52][53][53][53][55][55][55][55][56][56][57][57][57][58][62][62][63][64][66][66][67][67][67][67][67][67][69][69][69][69][69][71][72][74][76][76][76][77][78][78][79][81][82][85][87][87][89][89][90][91][92][93][93][98][101][101][101][103][104][105][107][107][107][109][110][110][111]

**note** : [58][98]

**noted** : [16][23][103]

**nothing** : [47][53][66][80][106]

**notice** : [36]

**notion** : [13][20][40]

**nourished** : [13]

**novelty** : [69]

**now** : [10][28][32][57][78][102][111]

**nowadays** : [80][83]

**nowhere** : [31]

**number** : [5][23][36]

**numerous** : [24][49]

**nutrients** : [48]

**nutrition** : [48]

# Letter O

**object** : [56][67]

**obliges** : [5]

**observe** : [32][54]

**obsession** : [59]

**obsolete** : [37]

**obstacle** : [12]

**occasions** : [79][106]

**occurs** : [104]

**October** : [1]

**of** : [0][0][0][1][1][2][2][2][2][2][2][2]
[3][3][3][4][4][4][5][5][5][5][6][6][6][6]
[6][7][7][7][7][7][7][7][7][8][8][8][8][8]
[9][9][10][10][10][10][10][10][10][10]
[10][11][11][11][11][11][12][12][12][12]
[12][12][12][12][12][12][12][12][13][13]
[13][13][13][13][14][14][14][14][14][14]
[14][14][15][15][15][15][15][15][15][15]
[15][16][16][16][16][16][16][16][16][17]
[17][17][17][17][17][17][17][17][17][18]
[18][18][18][18][18][18][19][19][19][19]
[19][19][19][19][19][20][20][20][20][20]
[20][20][20][20][20][21][21][21][22][22]
[22][22][22][22][22][22][22][22][22][22]
[22][22][23][23][23][23][23][24][24][24]
[25][25][25][25][25][25][26][26][26][26]
[26][26][26][26][26][26][27][27][28][29]
[29][30][30][30][30][30][30][30][30][30]
[30][30][30][30][30][31][31][32][32][32]
[32][32][32][32][33][33][33][33][33][33]
[33][33][33][33][33][33][34][34][34][35]
[35][35][35][35][36][36][36][36][36][36]
[37][37][37][37][37][37][37][38][38][38]
[38][38][38][39][39][39][39][39][39][39]
[40][40][40][40][40][40][40][40][41][41]
[41][41][41][42][42][42][42][42][42][42]
[42][42][42][43][43][43][43][43][43][43]
[43][43][43][43][43][43][43][43][44][44]
[44][44][44][45][45][45][45][45][45][46]
[46][46][46][46][47][47][47][47][48][48]
[48][48][48][48][48][48][48][48][48][48]
[48][48][48][48][48][49][49][49][49][49]
[49][49][50][50][50][50][50][51][51][51]
[52][52][52][52][52][52][52][52][52][52]
[53][53][54][54][54][54][55][55][56][56]
[57][57][57][57][58][58][58][58][58][58]
[59][59][59][60][60][60][60][61][61][61]
[62][62][62][62][62][63][63][64][64][64]
[65][65][65][65][65][65][65][65][66][66]
[66][66][66][66][66][66][66][66][66][67]
[67][67][67][68][68][68][68][68][68][68]
[69][69][69][69][69][69][69][70][70][70]
[70][70][70][70][70][70][70][70][71][71]
[71][71][71][71][72][72][72][72][72][72]
[72][72][73][73][73][73][73][73][74][74]
[74][74][74][74][75][75][75][75][75][75]
[75][75][76][76][76][77][77][77][78][78]
[78][78][78][78][79][79][79][80][80][80]
[81][81][81][81][81][82][82][82][82][82]
[82][83][83][83][84][84][84][84][84][84]
[85][85][85][85][85][85][86][86][86][86]
[86][87][87][87][87][87][87][87][87][87]
[88][88][88][88][88][88][88][89][89][89]
[89][89][89][90][90][91][92][92][92][92]
[93][93][93][93][93][93][94][94][94][94]
[94][94][94][95][95][95][95][95][96][96]
[96][96][96][96][96][97][97][97][98][98]
[98][99][99][99][100][100][101][101]
[101][101][101][101][101][101][101]

[102][102][102][102][103][104][104]
[105][105][106][106][106][107][107]
[107][107][107][108][108][108][108]
[108][108][108][109][109][109][109]
[110][110][110][110][111][111][111]
[111][111][111][111][111][111][111]
[111][111][111][111][111][111][111]
[111][111][111][111][111][111][111]

**off** : [15]

**offenses** : [19]

**offer** : [2][6][50][62][84]

**offering** : [21][105]

**officially** : [3]

**offspring** : [45]

**often** : [13][18][56][104][107]

**oil** : [14]

**older** : [30][34]

**on** : [1][6][8][8][11][11][12][20][26][27]
[27][30][32][33][39][42][43][43][47][48]
[48][48][50][52][52][53][56][65][67][68]
[68][68][74][78][80][81][82][83][89][94]
[97][98][99][103][104][104][105][109]
[111][111][111]

**once** :
[19][22][27][30][31][40][55][70][78]

**one** : [7][9][11][22][32][41][48][57][57]
[58][58][58][64][64][64][65][68][69][80]
[91][91][94][95][101][106][109][111]
[111]

**oneself** : [37]

**ongoing** : [90][93]

**onlookers** : [69]

**only** : [13][15][19][27][29][32][41][43]

[46][46][47][52][55][59][66][67][69][72]
[78][84][88][88][90][94][100]

**open** : [37][41][94][94][108]

**openness** : [69][70]

**opportunities** : [62]

**oppose** : [14]

**opposed** : [104]

**opposing** : [22]

**oppressed** : [19]

**oppression** : [22]

**opt** : [58][90]

**option** : [27][60][63]

**or** : [2][3][9][12][12][14][14][14][14]
[15][17][20][25][25][26][27][27][37][37]
[41][42][48][50][51][51][56][58][59][63]
[64][65][66][69][77][78][79][79][80][80]
[82][98][105][105][106][107][108]

**orally** : [34]

**ordained** : [93]

**order** : [11][33][51][105]

**ordered** : [87]

**orders** : [87][87][88][100][103]

**organization** : [85][103][104]

**organizations** : [24][50][62]

**organize** : [89]

**original** : [7][12][13][14][19][20][22]
[26][38][39][40][42][51][55][70][81]

**originally** : [78]

origins : [33]

other : [5][5][11][13][14][15][25][29]
[48][49][56][68][70][77][88][97][102]
[104][104][107][107]

others : [12][22][27][27][36][38][41]
[62][87][105][106][106][108]

otherwise : [27][52][104]

ought : [15][21][26][78][98]

our : [5][7][7][8][9][11][11][15][15][19]
[26][26][31][32][33][33][36][36][37][37]
[37][37][37][37][37][39][41][42][42][42]
[47][48][52][53][53][53][53][54][56][56]
[56][57][57][59][62][63][64][73][80][82]
[82][82][83][83][83][98][100][100][100]
[104][104][105][106][106][106][106]
[107][108][108][108][109][109][111]

ours : [5]

ourselves : [37][37][101][106][106]
[107]

out : [14][19][26][26][28][33][50][57]
[62][78][85][87][89][91][94][111]

outcast : [30]

outlet : [79]

outrage : [14][15]

outreach : [72][84]

outside : [76]

outskirts : [10][30][98]

over : [26][29][38][73][82][111]

overcome : [17][104]

overflow : [105]

overflowing : [105][111]

overflows : [43]

overlooked : [49]

overly : [69]

overwhelm : [52]

overwhelming : [7]

own : [2][5][12][21][27][31][32][32]
[33][37][37][39][40][45][51][51][56][59]
[77][78][106][106][106][108]

# Letter P

Pagan : [79]

Paganism : [78]

paid : [25]

pain : [111]

painful : [43][47]

pan : [97]

paper : [27]

paradigm : [46][52]

paradoxical : [43]

parliament : [9]

parrots : [9]

part : [6][25][48][48][50][55][62][74]
[85][95][103]

partial : [79][101][105]

participate : [26]

participation : [3][100]

**particular** : [14][35][49][68][69][81][87][94][104]

**particularly** : [41][51][84][89][97]

**parties** : [11]

**partners** : [26]

**parts** : [87]

**party** : [13][26]

**Paschal** : [74]

**passed** : [30][34][78][82]

**passes** : [46]

**passion** : [109]

**passionately** : [3]

**past** : [15][16]

**pastoral** : [75][78][84][85][90][98][104]

**pastors** : [4][60]

**path** : [45][111]

**paths** : [1][26][69][105][111]

**pathways** : [45]

**patriarch** : [44]

**Paul (as in Saint John Paul II)** : [67][87]

**pay** : [15]

**paying** : [15]

**peace** : [27][80][109]

**peasants** : [15]

**penalizing** : [14]

**pendular** : [98]

**penetrates** : [82]

**pennies** : [57]

**people** : [0][3][9][12][14][15][15][15][15][21][23][32][32][33][33][33][34][34][35][35][40][42][47][52][58][59][61][66][66][78][80][84][84][98]

**peoples** : [7][8][9][10][12][12][13][14][14][14][15][16][17][18][18][18][19][19][19][20][22][24][26][29][29][31][33][34][35][38][38][39][40][40][42][42][42][51][55][67][70][71][71][74][76][77][78][78][78][81][82][82][83][85][89][102][111][111]

**perform** : [92]

**perhaps** : [78][104]

**period** : [30]

**periods** : [86]

**permanent** : [92]

**permeates** : [20][74]

**permeating** : [24]

**permission** : [26]

**permit** : [94]

**perpetuate** : [37]

**perseveres** : [66]

**person** : [4][15][22][74]

**personal** : [20][20][35][65][71][73]

**person's** : [0][50][76][92][95]

**person's** : [59]

perspective : [104]

perspectives : [105]

Peru : [5]

Peruvian : [78]

petty : [111]

piece : [47][66]

pierced : [111]

piety : [78]

place : [15][26][26][37][40][43][49][51][68][68][95]

places : [16][30][42][77][85][89][94][99][104]

plain : [45]

plan : [27][98]

plane : [81][104]

planet : [48][53]

plant : [31][54]

planting : [74]

plants : [11][11]

play : [27][49][67][102][103]

plaything : [47]

plea : [8][19][57]

pleading : [52]

pleased : [35]

ploughshares : [46]

plunderers : [18]

plundering : [16]

poetry : [35][46][47]

poets : [46][46]

point : [25][33][33][48][96]

pointed : [78]

points : [30][76][108]

poisons : [24]

political : [17][58][62]

politicians : [14][50]

politics : [24][52]

pollute : [14][17][49]

pollution : [49]

polyhedron : [28]

pontificate : [111]

poor : [7][8][8][16][17][26][27][48][48][52][60][63][72][75][76][84][84][106][110][111]

popular : [46][78][78][89]

population : [10][30]

positions : [103]

possess : [35][78][107][107]

possessed : [12]

possesses : [31]

possessions : [71]

possibilities : [32]

possibility : [25]

possible : [17][38][61][79][94][108]

postmodern : [29]

post-synodal : [0]

potable : [14]

potentialities : [28]

pounds : [20]

pour : [105][111]

poured : [94]

pouring : [87]

pours : [89][91]

poverty : [10][16][30][63][75]

power : [13][38][42][52][52][68][87][87][88][88][101][101][101]

powerful : [48][52][111]

powers : [13]

practical : [93]

practices : [78]

pragmatic : [105]

praise : [50]

pray : [110]

prayed : [99]

prayer : [56][56][90]

preach : [62][64]

preached : [68]

preaching : [6][66][72]

precepts : [107]

precious : [35][55][72][109]

precisely : [25][27]

pre-Columbian : [70]

predecessor : [12]

preeminently : [90]

preference : [85]

preferential : [27]

preferred : [3]

pregnant : [15]

preparation : [111]

presence : [57][84][85][93][94][98][99]

present : [3][5][39][53][70][73][74][78][94][101][102]

presentation : [111]

presentations : [2]

presented : [11][12]

presenting : [26][80]

preservation : [48]

preserve : [7][7][13][21][21][50]

preserved : [37][99]

preserves : [71][104]

preserving : [49][51]

preside : [87]

presides : [91][101]

**pressure** : [50]

**presuming** : [66]

**presupposes** : [40]

**pretending** : [53]

**prevent** : [33][80]

**previously** : [30]

**prey** : [72]

**priest** : [87][87][87][87][87][88][88][99][101]

**priest's** : [88]

**priesthood** : [87]

**priestly** : [87][89][90][90][90]

**priests** : [18][90][92]

**primitive** : [34][43]

**principal** : [24][26][45][64][87]

**principally** : [87]

**prior** : [14][30]

**priorities** : [97]

**private** : [20]

**privatizing** : [14]

**privileged** : [61][81]

**privileges** : [22]

**probable** : [104]

**problems** : [3][5][23][62][80][85][104][105]

**process** : [2][2][33][40][66][68][68][69]

[71][72][78][78][79][93]

**processes** : [44]

**proclaim** : [89]

**proclaimed** : [65]

**proclaims** : [64]

**proclamation** : [61][64][64][64][96]

**production** : [53]

**professional** : [35]

**profit** : [14]

**profited** : [3][16]

**profits** : [52]

**profound** : [15][75]

**profoundly** : [99]

**programmes** : [62][93]

**progress** : [36]

**prohibits** : [42]

**project** : [11][40][65]

**projects** : [14][14][49][51][98]

**prolongation** : [20]

**promise** : [18]

**promote** : [8][28][39][90][93]

**promotion** : [106]

**prompted** : [99]

**proper** : [40][50][68][82][102][106]

**properly** : [101]

prophecy : [52][95]

prophetic : [8][19][27]

prophets : [46]

proposal : [97]

proposals : [25][26][42]

propose : [2][6][37][51][104]

proposes : [22]

proposing : [67]

protect : [11][37][51]

protected : [18]

protection : [19][52][60]

protests : [14]

prove : [36][48]

provenance : [25]

provide : [48]

provided : [30][42][98]

provoke : [15]

provoking : [9]

Ps (as in the Book of Psalms) : [15]

public : [50][103]

Puebla : [61]

pulled : [47]

pulsing : [45][111]

purchased : [9]

pure : [45]

purification : [79]

pursuit : [22][109]

puts : [43]

# Letter Q

qualifies : [87]

quality : [23][40][40][71]

queen : [43][111]

Querida (as in *Querida Amazonia*) : [0]

question : [26][93]

questions : [8][58][80]

quick : [14][78]

quite : [29][48]

# Letter R

racking : [15]

radiant : [57]

raft : [31]

rain : [48]

raised : [27]

raises : [43]

ranchers : [11]

range : [45]

ranks : [30]
raped : [15]

rare : [43]

rather : [10][50][66][78][84][84][87]

raw : [12]

ray : [45][107]

raze : [14]

razed : [15]

razing : [13]

reach : [82]

reached : [48]

reaches : [45][48]

read : [2][3][107]

readily : [36]

real : [10][103][104]

realities : [36][66]

reality : [20][41][59][104][104][111]

realization : [53]

realize : [49][69][101]

realizes : [91]

really : [48][53]

reason : [6][25][37][42][52][82][88][111]

reasons : [54][57][84]

receding : [43]

receive : [51][63][68]

received : [62][63][78][87][88][107]

receives : [68]

recent : [10][35]

reception : [2][68]

receptive : [77]

receptivity : [83]

recognition : [103]

recognize : [36][70][71]

recognizes : [12]

recognizing : [62][105]

recounted : [18]

recover : [35][70]

redeemed : [22]

redeemer : [74][107]

redemption : [67]

reductionism : [100]

re-educated : [72]

reference : [30]

refers : [87]

reflect : [107]

reflected : [67][85]

reflection : [2]

reflects : [32][103]

refused : [84]

regard : [15][37][50][58][71]

region : [1][1][2][3][4][4][5][6][7][7][7]

[7][8][8][10][10][11][12][12][15][15]
[15][16][18][19][20][24][24][26][26][26]
[28][29][31][32][33][35][36][38][40][41]
[41][41][42][43][46][48][48][48][48][49]
[50][51][52][55][55][56][57][57][57][58]
[60][61][61][61][62][64][65][66][69][70]
[70][71][75][76][78][78][81][84][85][89]
[90][92][94][95][96][98][98][99][102]
[102][105][106][107][108][110][110]
[111][111][111][111][111]

**regions** : [45]

**region's** : [16]

**regularly** : [92]

**regulate** : [23]

**reign** : [111][111][111]

**reigns** : [74]

**reiterate** : [68]

**reject** : [37]

**rejecting** : [37]

**rejects** : [66]

**relate** : [42][51]

**related** : [12][23][54]

**relations** : [22][38][97]

**relationship** : [22][31][41][73][73][74]

**relationships** : [14][20][20][23]

**relatively** : [23]

**relativizing** : [105]

**relaxation** : [83]

**religions** : [106][107][107]
**religiosity** : [76]

**religious** : [78][79][79][92][107]

**remain** : [40][42][85][108]

**remained** : [18]

**remaining** : [104]

**remarkable** : [99]

**remarkably** : [105]

**remember** : [18][56]

**reminded** : [17][67]

**remote** : [85][89]

**remotest** : [86]

**renewed** : [60][70]

**repeat** : [11][19]

**replace** : [2]

**replaced** : [48]

**reports** : [2]

**represent** : [36]

**representatives** : [24]

**reproach** : [73]

**reptiles** : [49]

**require** : [20]

**required** : [85]

**requires** : [49][92][94][94][102]

**reread** : [64]

**reshapes** : [66]
**resolute** : [75]

**resolve** : [80]

**resolved** : [104]

**resort** : [14]

**resound** : [61][64]

**resource** : [42][48]

**resources** : [12][48][48][50][52][62][71]

**respect** : [14][26][27][40][41][42][67][71][82]

**respectful** : [58][78]

**respond** : [57][62][79]

**responds** : [76]

**response** : [2][65][85][104]

**responsibilities** : [20][92]

**responsibility** : [50][50][70]

**responsible** : [71]

**responsive** : [102]

**rest** : [20][26][56][83]

**restore** : [22]

**restoring** : [17]

**restrict** : [100]

**result** : [24][27][37][39][48][52][55][78][101]

**results** : [23]

**resurrection** : [43][109]

**retrieval** : [72]

**return** : [18]

**reveal** : [75][76][84][101]

**revealed** : [64]

**reveals** : [57][111]

**revelation** : [68]

**revised** : [90]

**revival** : [38]

**rich** : [13][48][70][92]

**richer** : [13][106]

**riches** : [6][7][16][68][69][70]

**richness** : [31][35][37][39][66]

**rifles** : [46]

**right** : [14][51][54][64]

**rights** : [7][12][12][14][40][63][75][96]

**rise** : [10][27][77]

**risen** : [57][64][74][111]

**rises** : [9][43]

**risk** : [35][38][69]

**risks** : [48][51]

**rites** : [20]

**rituals** : [82]

**river** : [9][11][31][31][31][32][44][45][45][46][47][47][47][47][74][111]

**rivers** : [7][30][43][43][45][111]

**robs** : [46]

**rock** : [45]

role : [27][49][67][102][103]

roman : [3]

Rome : [1][111]

room : [20][84]

root : [66][68]

rooted : [58]

roots : [30][31][32][33][33][33][33][35][37][105]

rope : [47]

rubber : [15][46]

rules : [84]

running : [45]

rushing : [45]

# Letter S

sacrament : [87][88][89][91]

sacramental : [88]

sacraments : [81][81][84][88][89][107]

sacred : [5][70][73][79][107][107][110]

sad : [63]

sadism : [15]

sadly : [58]

said : [41][57][87]

sail : [15]

Saint (as in Saint John Paul II) : [67]

[87]

Saint (as in the Cathedral of Saint John Lateran) : [65]

Saint (as in Saint Joseph Anchieta) : [65]

Saint (as in Saint Turibius) : [65]

sake : [11][26]

salvation : [63][68]

same : [3][9][12][17][19][32][32][67][72][73][76][80][90][107][107]

sanctifies : [101]

Santarem : [61]

santo : [61]

satisfied : [52]

savages : [29]

save : [46][111]

Saviour : [109]

say : [88][89][108]

scattering : [46]

scenario : [30]

scenes : [15]

scientific : [52]

scorn : [66]

scourge : [14][24]

Scripture : [107]

scruple : [56]
seated : [26]

second : [45][82]

sectors : [35]

see : [32][35][53][54][63][66][68][75][78][80][105]

seed : [46][74]

seek : [26][79][89][105][108]

seem : [37]

seen : [31][35]

sees : [54][73][98]

seething : [35]

self-destructive : [53][108]

self-determination : [14]

selfishness : [108]

self-serving : [42]

sends : [109]

sensation : [47]

sense : [17][19][20][21][30][35][36][37][50][56][70][70][71][82][107][111]

sensibilities : [86]

sensitive : [15]

sensitivity : [95]

sentimental : [84]

serene : [58]

serenity : [21]

serious : [48][53]
serves : [48][53]

service : [63][77][86][88][93][95][102]

services : [103][103]

serving : [71]

set : [52][62][84][109][111]

sets : [3]

setting : [14][41]

seven : [107]

seventh : [111]

sexual : [10]

shade : [56]

shadows : [73]

shame : [19]

shameful : [15]

shamelessly : [39]

shape : [105]

shaped : [65][78]

shaping : [87]

share : [60][72][107]

shared : [5][20][20][37][37][47][70]

sharing : [111]

she : [19][56][59][66][66][66][66][66][67][70][72]

shedding : [96]

shelters : [13]

shimmering : [44][45]

**so-called** : [19]

**social** : [7][8][15][22][23][24][24][25][26][35][39][39][40][41][58][59][63][74][75][75][76][76][85][96]

**society** : [20][20][24][50][102]

**society's** : [23]

**softly** : [20]

**soil** : [31][48][48]

**sold** : [57]

**sole** : [107]

**solidarity** : [17][17][22][70]

**solitude** : [77]

**solution** : [62]

**solutions** : [104][105][105][105]

**some** : [2][4][35][38][49][53][79][79][85][99][107][107]

**someone** : [56][80]

**something** : [28][32][35][56][69][78][83][107]

**sometimes** : [31]

**son** : [74][101][111][111]

**song** : [56][82]

**songs** : [42]

**sons** : [57][111]

**sort** : [13]

**sought** : [17]
**souls** : [79]

**sound** : [58]

**source** : [12][34][35][71][87][88][92]

**sources** : [17][49]

**south** : [97]

**sower** : [46]

**sown** : [68]

**sows** : [46]

**space** : [12][57][66]

**spaces** : [45]

**sparrows** : [57]

**spatter** : [47]

**speak** : [6][62][72][88][106]

**speaking** : [99]

**speaks** : [24][63]

**special** : [25][75][94][95]

**species** : [49][49][54][54][54]

**specific** : [69][85][87][89][94][102]

**spells** : [47]

**spinal** : [45]

**Spirit (as in the Holy Spirit)** : [20][68][68][68][69][69][89][91][94][99][106][108][109]

**Spirit's (as in the Holy Spirit)** : [94]

**spirit** : [20][109]

**spiritual** : [60][74][76][76][79][93][94][108]

subjecting : [14]

subjection : [10]

subjects : [39]

suborning : [14]

subside : [43]

subtly : [100]

such : [14][16][23][41][53][54][80][84]
[86][100]

suffer : [109][111]

suffering : [3][16][18][46][46]

sufferings : [15]

sufficient : [76]

sufficiently : [98]

suitable : [75][92]

suited : [17]

summary : [64]

summer : [43][43]

summit : [88][92]

summons : [57][100]

Sunday : [83][83][86]

superabundant : [7]

superficial : [53]

superior : [87]

supernatural : [81]

superstition : [78]

support : [71][98]

supportive : [28]

supposedly : [36]

supposes : [68]

supremely : [108]

surely : [41][45]

surface : [48]

Surinam : [5]

surprised : [56]

surrounding : [20]

surroundings : [13][31][32][44]

survival : [49]

survive : [12][13][29]

survived : [31]

survivors : [17]

sustain : [101]

sustainable : [17][51][58]

sustained : [30]

sustains : [73]

swallowed : [108]

swell : [30][43]

swells : [45]

swept : [45]

syllables : [44]
symbiosis : [31]

**testimony** : [99]

**text** : [2]

**texts** : [107]

**than** : [3][12][15][20][28][35][48][66]
[78][84][106]

**thank** : [19]

**thanks** : [31][35]

**that** : [1][2][2][2][2][4][5][5][6][6][6][6]
[7][7][7][8][8][8][8][8][9][9][11][12][12]
[12][13][13][14][14][15][15][16][16][17]
[17][17][17][18][18][18][18][18][19][19]
[19][19][20][20][22][23][24][25][25][26]
[28][28][28][29][29][30][30][30][31][33]
[33][34][34][35][35][35][35][36][37][37]
[37][37][39][39][40][40][41][41][41][41]
[41][42][43][43][45][45][45][45][45][46]
[46][46][47][47][47][48][48][48][48][48]
[49][49][49][50][51][52][53][53][53][54]
[55][55][56][56][57][58][58][61][62][62]
[63][63][63][63][63][64][64][64][64][65]
[65][66][66][67][67][67][68][68][68][68]
[68][69][69][69][69][69][71][71][71][73]
[73][73][73][74][75][76][76][76][78][78]
[78][78][78][79][80][82][84][84][84][84]
[86][87][87][87][87][87][87][88][88][88]
[88][89][89][89][89][90][90][91][91][91]
[91][92][92][93][93][94][94][94][95][98]
[99][100][100][101][101][101][102]
[102][103][103][103][103][103][104]
[104][105][105][105][105][105][105]
[105][106][106][106][107][107][107]
[107][107][107][108][109][109][109]
[109][109][109][111][111][111][111]
[111][111][111][111][111][111]

**the** : [0][0][1][1][1][1][1][1][1][2][2][2]
[2][2][2][2][2][2][2][3][3][3][3][3][3][3]
[3][3][4][4][4][4][4][4][5][5][5][5][5][5]
[6][6][6][6][6][7][7][7][7][7][7][7][7][8]
[8][8][8][8][8][8][8][9][9][9][9][9][9]
[9][9][9][9][9][10][10][10][10][10][10]
[10][10][10][10][10][10][10][11][11][11]

[11][11][11][11][11][11][11][11][11][11]
[12][12][12][12][12][12][12][12][12][12]
[12][12][12][12][12][12][13][13][13][13]
[13][13][13][13][13][13][13][13][14][14]
[14][14][14][14][14][14][14][14][14][14]
[15][15][15][15][15][15][15][15][15][15]
[15][15][15][15][15][15][15][15][15][16]
[16][16][16][16][16][16][16][16][16][16]
[16][16][16][17][17][17][17][17][17][17]
[17][17][17][17][17][18][18][18][18][18]
[18][18][18][18][18][18][18][18][18][19]
[19][19][19][19][19][19][19][19][19][19]
[19][19][19][19][19][19][19][19][19][19]
[20][20][20][20][20][20][20][20][20][20]
[20][20][20][20][20][21][21][21][21][22]
[22][22][22][22][22][22][22][22][22][22]
[23][23][23][23][23][24][24][24][24][24]
[24][24][25][25][25][25][25][26][26][26]
[26][26][26][26][26][26][26][26][27][27]
[27][27][27][27][27][27][27][28][28][28]
[28][29][29][29][30][30][30][30][30][30]
[30][30][30][30][30][30][30][30][30][30]
[30][31][31][31][31][31][31][31][31][32]
[32][32][32][32][32][32][32][33][33][33]
[33][33][33][33][33][33][33][33][34][34]
[34][34][34][35][35][35][35][35][36][36]
[36][36][36][37][37][37][37][37][37][37]
[38][38][39][39][39][39][39][39][39][40]
[40][40][40][40][40][40][40][40][40][40]
[41][41][41][41][41][41][41][41][41][41]
[41][41][41][42][42][42][42][42][42][42]
[42][42][42][42][42][42][42][42][42][42]
[43][43][43][43][43][43][43][43][43][43]
[43][43][43][43][43][43][43][43][43][43]
[43][43][43][43][43][44][44][44][44][44]
[45][45][45][45][45][45][45][45][45][45]
[45][45][45][45][45][45][45][45][45][45]
[45][45][45][45][46][46][46][46][46][46]
[46][46][46][46][46][47][47][47][47][47]
[47][47][47][47][48][48][48][48][48][48]
[48][48][48][48][48][48][48][48][48][48]
[48][48][48][48][48][48][48][48][48][48]
[48][48][48][48][48][49][49][49][49][49]
[49][49][50][50][50][50][50][51][51][51]
[51][51][52][52][52][52][52][52][52][52]
[52][52][52][52][52][52][52][53][53][53]
[54][54][55][55][55][55][55][55][55][56]
[56][56][56][56][56][56][57][57][57][57]
[57][57][57][57][57][57][58][58][58][58]

[58][59][59][59][59][59][60][60][60][60]
[60][60][60][60][61][61][61][61][61][61]
[61][61][61][61][61][62][62][62][62][62]
[62][62][63][63][63][63][63][63][63][63]
[63][63][64][64][64][64][64][64][64][64]
[64][64][64][64][65][65][65][65][65][65]
[65][65][65][65][65][65][65][65][65][65]
[66][66][66][66][66][66][66][66][66][66]
[66][66][66][66][66][66][66][66][66][66]
[67][67][67][67][67][67][67][68][68][68]
[68][68][68][68][68][68][68][68][68][68]
[68][68][68][68][68][69][69][69][69][69]
[69][69][69][69][69][69][69][69][69][70]
[70][70][70][70][70][70][70][70][70][70]
[70][70][70][70][70][71][71][71][71][71]
[71][71][71][72][72][72][72][72][72][72]
[72][72][73][73][73][73][73][73][73][73]
[73][73][73][74][74][74][74][74][74][74]
[74][74][74][74][74][74][74][74][74][74]
[75][75][75][75][75][75][75][75][75][75]
[75][76][76][76][76][76][76][76][76][76]
[76][76][76][77][77][78][78][78][78][78]
[78][78][78][78][79][80][80][80][80][80]
[80][81][81][81][81][81][81][81][81][81]
[81][82][82][82][82][82][82][82][82][82]
[82][83][83][83][83][83][84][84][84][84]
[84][84][84][84][84][85][85][85][85][85]
[85][85][85][85][86][86][86][86][86][86]
[87][87][87][87][87][87][87][87][87][87]
[87][87][87][87][87][87][87][87][87][87]
[87][87][87][87][87][88][88][88][88][88]
[88][88][88][88][88][89][89][89][89][89]
[89][89][89][89][89][89][89][89][90][90]
[90][90][90][91][91][91][91][91][91][91]
[91][92][92][92][92][92][93][94][94][94]
[94][94][94][94][94][94][94][94][94][94]
[94][95][95][95][95][95][96][96][96][96]
[96][96][97][97][97][97][97][97][97][97]
[98][98][98][98][98][98][98][98][99][99]
[99][99][99][99][100][100][100][101]
[101][101][101][101][101][101][101]
[101][101][101][101][101][101][101]
[101][101][101][101][102][102][102]
[102][102][102][103][103][103][103]
[103][104][104][104][104][104][105]
[105][105][105][105][105][106][106]
[106][106][106][106][106][107][107]
[107][107][107][107][107][107][107]
[108][108][108][108][109][109][109]

[109][109][109][109][109][109][109]
[109][109][110][110][110][110][110]
[111][111][111][111][111][111][111]
[111][111][111][111][111][111][111]
[111][111][111][111][111][111][111]
[111][111][111][111][111][111][111]
[111][111][111][111][111][111][111]
[111][111][111][111][111]

**their** : [5][5][7][7][10][12][12][12][12]
[14][15][15][15][17][18][18][18][20][20]
[20][20][20][20][21][21][21][23][24][26]
[26][26][26][29][31][32][32][33][34][34]
[35][35][35][35][36][36][37][39][40][41]
[42][42][51][51][51][51][51][53][54][54]
[57][57][63][63][71][72][72][74][76][78]
[78][80][80][82][89][95][95][96][96][96]
[99][99][99][100][101][103][107][111]
[111]

**theirs** : [101][101][103]

**them** : [5][8][12][12][13][13][17][17]
[18][18][21][21][23][26][27][30][30][30]
[33][33][33][36][40][53][53][57][57][57]
[63][63][63][63][63][67][72][72][72][72]
[72][72][73][76][78][79][80][83][84][99]
[101][101][101][105]

**themselves** : [13][14][26][32][35][39]
[42][42][72]

**then** : [23][31][31][32][35][40][45][48]
[50][52][55][87][89][92][106]

**theological** : [57]

**there** : [3][10][11][11][16][20][24][28]
[30][31][33][35][39][40][41][41][43][45]
[45][45][49][50][51][69][84][86][87][88]
[92][94][99][101][105][111][111]

**thermometer** : [43]

**these** : [12][17][21][21][21][33][43][45]
[50][57][62][70][71][72][72][82][88]
[103]

**they** : [3][3][3][9][10][12][12][12][14]

[14][15][15][15][15][15][15][18][18][20]
[21][24][26][26][29][29][29][29][30][30]
[32][33][35][35][35][42][42][46][51][52]
[54][58][61][63][63][63][64][69][69][71]
[71][71][71][71][71][78][81][81][81][84]
[84][89][96][100][100][104][105][107]
[111]

**thick** : [45]

**thin** : [47]

**thing** : [28][83]

**things** : [31][47][53][59][71][71][74]
[74][76][105]

**think** : [20][53][69][87][106]

**thinking** : [47][105]

**third** : [11]

**this** : [1][2][2][3][5][6][6][8][10][12]
[13][13][14][17][21][22][22][25][26][27]
[27][28][30][32][33][33][35][35][37][37]
[40][41][41][41][42][42][42][45][46][46]
[47][48][49][50][52][53][55][56][57][58]
[60][61][61][64][64][65][65][66][66][68]
[68][69][70][71][71][71][72][72][73][73]
[74][75][75][76][76][77][78][82][82][82]
[82][83][83][83][83][87][87][87][88][88]
[89][89][89][90][90][92][94][94][95][97]
[98][99][100][101][101][101][102][103]
[104][105][105][105][106][107][107]
[108][108][108][109][110][111][111]
[111][111][111][111]

**thorough** : [51]

**thoroughly** : [90]

**those** : [9][10][14][18][18][21][21][23]
[26][26][31][32][32][33][34][34][37][42]
[43][46][47][51][58][62][62][68][72][72]
[75][76][78][78][87][90][90][92][98][99]
[102][103][109]

**thou** : [73][73]

**though** : [8][47][73][99][102][107][107]
[111]

**thought** : [47][69][98]

**thousand** : [9]

**thousands** : [32][54][54]

**threading** : [45]

**threat** : [28][38][59]

**threatened** : [11]

**threatening** : [48][48]

**threats** : [12][102]

**three** : [40]

**through** : [45][45][66][66][72][72][75]
[82][93][94][97][99][101][101][111]

**throughout** : [15][19][60]

**thus** : [51][55][76]

**tight** : [47]

**timber** : [9][9][11][11][14][49]

**time** : [3][17][19][34][45][53][66][67]
[73][76][80][86][90][105][107]

**times** : [25][29][30][79][107][108]

**to** : [0][0][2][2][2][2][2][2][2][2][3][3]
[3][4][5][5][5][5][5][6][6][8][8][8][9][9]
[9][10][11][11][11][11][12][12][12][12]
[12][12][12][13][13][13][13][13][14][14]
[14][14][14][14][14][14][15][15][15][15]
[15][15][15][15][15][15][15][15][16][16]
[17][17][17][17][17][17][17][17][18][18]
[18][19][19][19][20][21][21][21][21][21]
[21][21][21][22][22][22][22][23][24][25]
[25][25][25][25][26][26][26][26][26][26]
[26][26][27][27][27][28][28][28][28][28]

transient : [27]

transmission : [30][39]

transparency : [19]

trap : [101]

traps : [104]

traversed : [34]

treasure : [29][36][107][107][107]

treated : [2]

treating : [47]

treats : [56]

tree : [66]

trees : [9][11][31][31][46][46][47][74]

tried : [46]

tries : [37]

tropic : [45]

trouble : [29]

troubles : [10]

true : [8][8][24][41][45][69][74][74][74][76][108]

truly : [46][89]

trust : [41][94][111]

truth : [37][47][107]

try : [79][106]

trying : [35][53][53]
Turibius (as in Saint Turibius of

Mogrovejo) : [65]

turn : [33][41][73]

turned : [46][46]

turning : [82][111]

turns : [48][84]

twenty : [15]

two : [27][57][76][88][101][104]

typical : [20][58][95]

typically : [101]

# Letter U

umbilical : [34]

unaffected : [40]

unceasingly : [65]

uncivilized : [29]

unconcerned : [85]

uncritically : [37]

under : [28]

undergoes : [68]

underground : [45]

understand : [86]

understanding : [78][84][100]

understands : [41]

understood : [40][98]

undoubtedly : [99]

**unduly** : [14]

**unequal** : [43]

**unethical** : [14]

**uneven** : [85]

**unexpected** : [105]

**unfair** : [32]

**unique** : [31]

**unite** : [81]

**united** : [91][109][109][109][109][109][109][109]

**unites** : [45][108][108][108][110]

**unity** : [45][91][91]

**universal** : [77]

**universe** : [31][57][74]

**unless** : [58][58][84]

**unlike** : [37]

**unnecessary** : [83]

**unprecedented** : [102]

**unproductive** : [83]

**unrealistic** : [37]

**unrest** : [59]

**unscrupulous** : [16]

**unseen** : [49]

**unsettling** : [21]

**untouched** : [45]

**up** : [9][10][14][15][22][24][27][31][33][45][69][69][71][74][79][80][81][82][84][89][98][108][109][111]

**upon** : [44][45][67][87][91][111]

**uprooted** : [21]

**uprootedness** : [21]

**uprooting** : [28]

**urban** : [21][36][72][72][98]

**urge** : [33][90]

**urgent** : [52][90]

**us** : [1][2][5][11][15][15][15][18][19][20][22][22][26][32][37][40][41][41][41][41][45][45][45][46][46][47][52][52][52][54][54][55][55][55][56][56][56][57][57][63][63][64][64][65][69][69][71][71][72][73][73][77][78][78][81][82][99][100][100][100][101][102][104][105][105][108][108][108][108][108][108][109][109][109][109][109][109][109][110][111][111][111][111]

**use** : [55]

**used** : [14][56][79]

**useful** : [104]

**using** : [13][31]

**usually** : [30]

**usurpers** : [12]

**utterly** : [14]

# Letter V

**valid** : [104]

valuable : [72]

value : [5][51][54][60][83][100][108]

valued : [71]

values : [21][30][37][39][70][70]

varied : [7][32][66][78]

variety :
[6][33][48][49][64][91][92][93]

various : [17][26][35][42][93][97]

vast : [9][45][85]

Vatican (as in the Second Vatican Council) : [82]

vegetation : [48][48]

vein : [47]

veins : [42][43]

Venezuela : [5]

Venezuelan : [15]

verifiable : [42]

version : [14]

very : [29][42][54][57][83][84][93][104]

vices : [53]

victims : [24]

view : [22]

viewed : [12][29][81]

vigorous : [94]

violations : [14]

violence : [18][23][59]

visible : [49]

vision : [33][100][100][105]

visions : [38]

vital : [32][111]

vitality : [80]

Vivit (as in Christus Vivit) : [64]

vocation : [90]

vocations : [90]

voice : [26][27][46][47][70]

voices : [7][11][56]

voluntary : [29]

# Letter W

wall : [37]

want : [80]

wants : [73]

warm : [107]

warming : [48]

was : [11][16][18][19][30][31][31][47]

waste : [58]

watchful : [67]
water : [14][20][35][42][42][43][43][44][44][45][45][45][47][49]

watering : [106]

waters : [43][43][45][45][45][73]

**waterways** : [11]

**way** : [4][6][13][14][17][21][22][35][37]
[42][47][53][64][66][68][70][72][74][75]
[76][77][79][81][81][84][86][87][89][94]
[99][101][101][103][105][105][108]

**ways** : [7][12][27][37][64][64][66][85]
[89][98][104][111][111]

**we** : [8][11][11][11][11][14][15][17][17]
[18][18][18][19][21][21][21][24][25][26]
[26][26][26][26][27][32][33][36][37][37]
[41][42][42][42][50][53][53][54][54][55]
[55][55][55][56][56][56][56][57][57][58]
[62][62][62][62][63][63][63][63][63][63]
[64][64][64][66][68][69][69][69][70][72]
[73][73][75][76][76][78][82][82][83][83]
[85][85][85][85][89][89][91][93][93][98]
[100][101][101][102][104][106][106]
[106][106][106][107][107][107][107]
[107][107][107][107][108][108][108]
[108][109][109][109][109][109][109]
[109][109][110][110][111][111][111]
[111][111]

**weak** : [13][75]

**weakening** : [28]

**weakens** : [23]

**weaker** : [36]

**weather** : [43][59]

**weep** : [56]

**welcomed** : [72]

**welcomes** : [91]

**welcoming** : [98]

**well** : [10][12][19][25][35][36][45][53]
[98]

**welling** : [22]

**wellspring** : [88]

**were** : [12][12][12][12][13][15][15][15]
[18][18][25][29][47][63][76][86][93]
[100]

**western** : [36]

**what** : [14][26][28][33][41][65][68][68]
[69][87][87][87][100][104][108][108]
[108][108][108][108][111]

**wheat** : [19][78]

**when** : [14][14][15][31][37][41][42][43]
[48][49][59][65][68][87][88][96][104]
[106]

**whenever** : [68]

**where** : [7][7][9][10][20][24][38][41]
[42][45][57][58][77][104][109]

**whereas** : [11][13]

**wherever** : [94]

**which** : [1][3][3][5][12][13][14][15][17]
[18][20][22][23][23][24][24][30][31][33]
[33][34][36][37][40][41][41][42][46][48]
[48][50][52][54][54][55][57][60][64][64]
[64][66][66][66][69][72][76][81][81][83]
[83][87][89][91][98][101][105][105]
[107][107][107][107][111]

**while** : [9][13][13][16][29][45][51][63]
[67][71][72][74][80][103][104][106]
[108]

**white** : [45]

**who** : [3][11][14][16][16][18][18][18]
[21][26][32][32][32][33][34][35][35][41]
[41][43][47][51][57][62][62][63][64][68]
[69][69][72][72][73][73][74][74][75][75]
[80][80][84][84][86][87][90][91][93][98]
[98][99][101][103][106][109][109][109]
[109][111][111][111]

**whole** : [5][5][22][48][48][64][65][73][76]

**whom** : [26][26][26][92][111]

**whose** : [111]

**why** : [34][87][101]

**wild** : [12]

**will** : [0][2][4][9][20][26][33][35][36][40][46][53][54][54][54][55][56][56][57][58][75][75][76][77][79][79][80][101][105][106][106][107][109]

**wind** : [45][74]

**wings** : [20][69]

**winners** : [13]

**winter** : [43]

**wipe** : [109]

**wisdom** : [22][30][32][34][42][51][66][70][72][72]

**wish** : [2][2][26]

**wished** : [75]

**wishes** : [22][72]

**with** : [2][7][9][12][13][13][15][15][19][19][20][22][26][26][27][28][30][31][31][31][32][34][35][36][37][37][39][40][41][42][42][43][43][43][45][45][46][46][47][48][48][48][51][52][53][55][55][56][56][57][57][58][59][60][60][61][62][62][62][63][63][63][65][66][68][68][68][69][71][72][72][72][73][73][74][75][75][77][77][77][79][79][80][81][82][83][83][84][90][90][92][93][94][94][96][97][98][98][105][105][106][106][107][107][107][107][107][109][109][111][111][111][111]

**withhold** : [51]

**within** : [22][23][40][40][40][55][86]

**without** : [17][20][21][28][28][28][31][32][34][40][50][55][56][64][71][72][73][74][79][101][108]

**witness** : [66]

**witnessed** : [13]

**witnesses** : [77]

**witnessing** : [10]

**woe** : [62]

**woman** : [64][101]

**womanhood** : [103]

**womb** : [15][111]

**women** : [4][14][15][15][92][98][98][99][99][100][100][101][101][101][102][102][103][103][107][111]

**won** : [26]

**wonder** : [73][111]

**wood** : [73]

**woodlands** : [48]

**Word (as in Christ)** : [74]

**word** : [83][89][93][109][111]

**words** : [26][41][42][88][107]

**work** : [4][15][18][20][66][70][75][83][83][106][108][110][110]

**worked** : [66]

**workers** : [75][78][104]

working : [27][51][63][72]

works : [25]

world : [1][5][5][6][40][46][46][46][53][55][60][64][74][74][81][82][87][107][108]

worldview : [74]

worldviews : [32]

worms : [49]

worship : [70]

worst : [10]

worthy : [88]

would : [3][3][12][15][15][18][27][33][34][37][37][47][54][60][63][64][64][64][68][69][76][80][93][95][98][100][100][100][100][101][103]

wounds : [74][111]

writing : [35]

# Letter X

xenophobia : [10]

**XVI (as in Pope Benedict XVI)** : [12][41]

# Letter Y

year : [54][111]

yearnings : [76]

years : [35][78][82]

ye'kuana : [15][15]

yet : [5][11][17][18][28][46][49][54][57][62][87][104]

yields : [46]

you : [15][19][33][44][44][64][73][88][111][111][111][111][111]

young : [12][33][33][34][72][98]

your : [19][20][31][31][33][88][111][111][111][111]

# Letter Z

No Entries

May unseen work bear fruit for eternal life